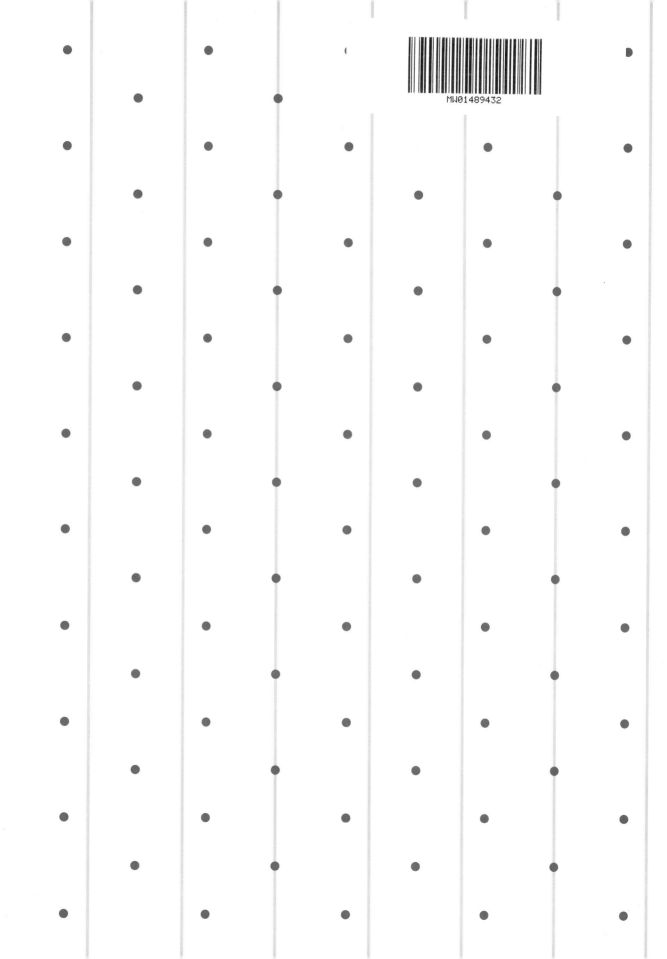

MW01489432

The Making of a Rag Doll

Design & Sew Modern Heirlooms

jess brown

photographs by tristan davison

CHRONICLE BOOKS

SAN FRANCISCO

Text and illustrations copyright © 2014 by Jess Brown.
Photographs copyright © 2014 by Tristan Davison.

All rights reserved. No part of this book may be reproduced
in any form without written permission from the publisher.

Library of Congress Cataloging-in-Publication Data available.

ISBN 978-1-4521-1951-9

Manufactured in China

Designed by Jennifer Tolo Pierce

10 9 8 7 6 5 4 3 2 1

Chronicle Books LLC
680 Second Street
San Francisco, California 94107
www.chroniclebooks.com

for erio, stella, and tiger,
the loves of my life

Contents

✳

Introduction

I have always adored rag dolls. Since I was a child, I've found that a doll, a truly loved doll, is the ultimate comfort. When I was growing up, there were beautiful rag dolls and patchwork quilts in my home. A family friend once brought me a rag doll from London. I think I was around four years old and I was completely enchanted by the doll's simplicity. I called her Frances. I didn't have many toys made from natural materials and it felt so good to hug this doll. I felt a special connection with it.

She was made of coarse-weave cotton muslin. You could see every thread of the fabric. She was stuffed with firm cotton fiber so her limbs kept their shape and she could sit upright. Her hair was made of wool yarn and her face was embroidered. She was wearing the most incredible dress made from a Liberty of London floral fabric that had a base of rich French blue sprinkled with red, pink, and cream flowers. The dress was embellished with dark blue satin on the bodice and fine lace trim around the hemline, and she had a small satin bow in her hair.

I kept her always. Frances was just one of those things I couldn't part with. In fact, she became my daughter's doll for a while and then eventually moved into my studio. I keep her where I can see her. This doll is a constant reminder of why I create.

As a little girl, before I even knew how to sew, I would make small cloth dolls out of scraps of fabric found around the house. I loved the feel of each different piece of fabric, and running my fingers across the embroidery of a rag doll's face. I'd make little doll accessories and houses out of shoeboxes. I loved creating a world out of discarded bits and pieces, and no doubt these early creative moments were formative. I still love working with well-worn textiles that tell a story. Antique cloth carries the tradition of the handwork artisan. Examining the individual threads and stitches in each fabric scrap brings me directly to each artist's hand. I get inspired thinking about how each piece of cloth was created, used well, and loved. From the simplest scrap of linen to the most ornate French embroidery, I see the beauty and promise in the threadbare, and try to honor the past in everything I make.

When my daughter was born, I wanted to fill her room with handmade toys and bedding. I searched shops to find things that would be both beautiful and useful. Sadly, I didn't see much that felt authentic. It was nearly impossible to find a product made in a truly artful way, especially for a child. I quickly realized that I would need to make my children's toys and bedding.

First I had a vision for the dolls. I wanted them to be unforgettable. Not just cute or durable, but truly unforgettable and distinctive. I knew I wanted to use organic stuffing. The density and smell of corn fiber felt real to me—solid, not spongy, but reminiscent of dolls made long ago. I wanted the doll to be soft to the touch, so it would feel good when my daughter hugged it close against her face. The hair on the doll's head would be soft and gentle, not a scratchy yarn, and the eyes would be created with the finest embroidery floss. I wanted the look and feel of a toy that was slightly more sophisticated and had personality—a gentle face that wasn't telling her how to look or feel, but was just there to give comfort.

The first doll I made was from what I can truly call a happy accident. When my daughter, Stella, was a baby, all of my cashmere sweaters were accidentally thrown in the washing machine. Ruined, they sat for months in a bag near my sewing machine. I just

couldn't bear to part with them. One day it just hit me: I could create a doll for Stella totally out of cashmere. I couldn't imagine a more perfect toy for a baby. I had no pattern to work with. I just had a general sense of how I wanted it to look and feel. It needed to have a quiet and calm sensibility. I knew I wanted it to be really pretty but not too precious. I loved the idea that this doll would be created with some of my favorite sweaters.

I remember struggling a bit on the design. First, I sewed the entire doll by hand. But when I was done, I realized the sweater body probably wouldn't hold up if she really fell in love with it. I went back and removed all of the stitches and sewed it up again on my machine. I sewed the arms and legs separately and stuffed them with a basic cotton fill. When I began to attach the limbs, I noticed I had stuffed them inside out. The seams were showing on the outside. I decided to just go with it and sewed them on as is. Little details like that gave the doll texture and told a story.

I used more cashmere cut into strips to create long hair, and I stitched the eyes. For the dress, I chose a small white antique napkin with crocheted lace details from my linens collection. The doll was perfect. Stella adored her. She was just learning to speak at the time. The doll was created using two different

The Making of a Rag Doll

shades of gray, and Stella named her Gracie. I have created many, many dolls for both of my children, but Gracie was the first, and definitely set a tone for the feeling I want to create in my dolls.

Three years later, when my son, Tiger, was born, I decided to do the same thing for him, filling his room with dolls and creatures made from the softest, most appealing fabrics.

A few years after making that first doll, a friend and I decided to open a children's shop on a shoestring budget. She planned to sell the beautiful clothes she made for children, and I brought in my rag dolls. I started with six dolls in the shop for our holiday sales. They went fast. I made another group and they also sold very quickly. Soon other shop owners came in and wanted to place doll orders for their shops. I began filling small orders, but it was important to me to absolutely love the stores where the dolls would be sold. I felt a deep commitment to seeing where the dolls would take me, and it has been wonderful to find that I am not the only one craving this type of product. Creating a modern heirloom that a child can hold, love, and pass on became my passion and I've been working at it ever since.

I wrote this book to share what I love and to inspire you to carry on the tradition of handmade heirlooms in your own unique way. I offer ways for finding fabrics and materials along with my favorite tools and techniques. I've included a pattern for an original Jess Brown Rag Doll design as well as patterns and instructions for a quilt, apron, knickers, dresses, hats, and other accessories. I'm thrilled to play a small role in keeping the tradition of the handmade alive.

My wish is that you bring to these projects your own vision, love, and passion. For it is these elements that make a true heirloom.

—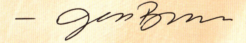

In My Studio

I love to work in natural light. My home studio is an enclosed sunporch with two walls of windows. I connect better with the textures and patterns in the fabrics I'm using if my work space gets lots of sunlight.

On my long, narrow table, my sewing machine sits at one end and all of my supplies are within reach. I like to see everything and have all materials and supplies at my fingertips while I'm working: jars of buttons and pom-poms, tins of lace trim, and open shelving filled with fabric. If I store my collections in drawers, I'll forget what I have! And the tools I use are close at hand. My favorite scissors, large and small, live in jars near my sewing machine. My measuring tape hangs on a hook nearby just above my pins, tailor's chalk, and pincushions filled with my favorite needles.

When not working at my machine, I like to work on the floor. I cut all of my patterns on the floor and I like to work on my quilts this way, too. It helps to stand above something you're working on so you can see it from all angles: it provides depth and perspective and makes it clear where you need more of one thing and less of another.

The Making of a Rag Doll

Getting started on any new piece, whether it's a doll, a quilt, or an item of clothing, requires inspiration. I am a true believer in surrounding myself entirely with things that inspire me. I have scraps pinned to walls, delicate bits of lace strung together hanging in a window, and antique dishes and bowls filled with buttons or bits of embroidery. Any direction my eye goes, it lands on something that speaks to my aesthetic vision and my creativity.

When I begin sewing I have a few little rituals. I always sew barefoot. Then I turn on some music that will engulf my space—anything from Édith Piaf to The Clash, depending on my mood. I love being totally wrapped up in my creativity. This is when I can really dig in. I pull out the fabrics that feel right to me and begin. I sketch out a drawing of an idea and then begin cutting fabric and pinning together the form I am imagining.

I generally work as though I'm creating a piece for one of my children, which keeps me deeply connected with each design and helps me make thoughtful, special choices. Just as I make dolls and quilts as heirlooms for my children to pass on, I try to create this sentiment for other families as well.

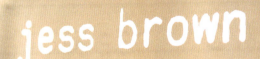

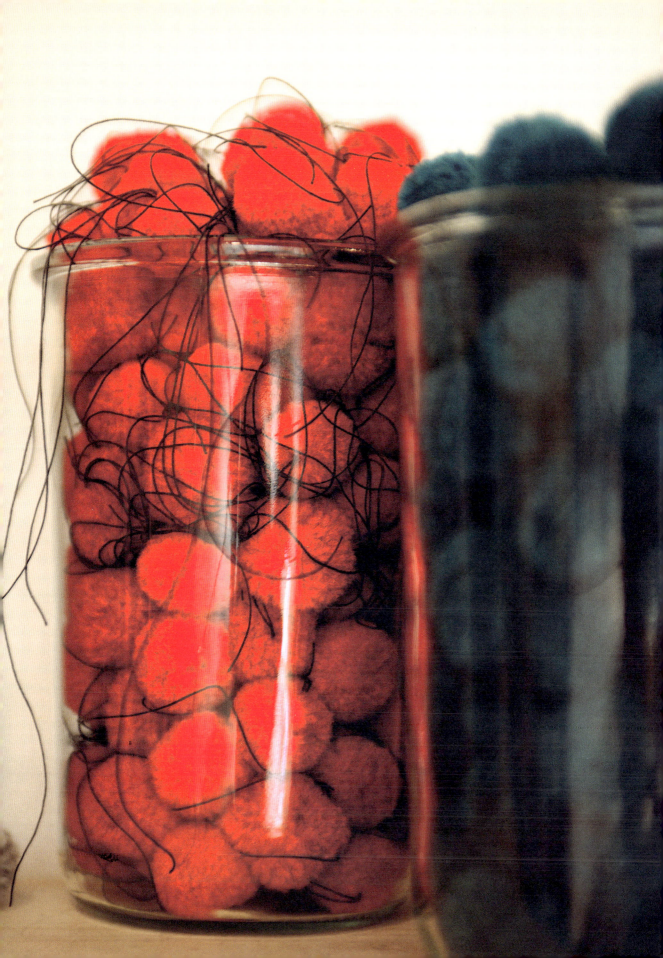

Creating the Doll

When I was first designing the Jess Brown Rag Doll, the most challenging part of the process was deciding on the personality and look of the doll. Once I had the form of the doll, I struggled with how to keep it true to my aesthetic. It was important to me to keep the doll sophisticated.

DETAILS

The face seemed central to me. After embroidering several different types of eyes, I decided on the star shape. With these starry eyes, the doll's face seemed to light up. The mouth was a defining element of the doll. The shape and color of the mouth create expression, and a small heart shape felt just right. The simplicity of the star eyes and heart-shaped mouth stitched in a subtle color palette created the warmth I was after. There is a definite sweetness about the face, but also a timeless sophistication. I wanted people to look at this doll and not necessarily know which era it came from.

The length of the doll was also a challenge. The basic rag doll that I make is 22 in/56 cm long. This came about in the most practical way. When my daughter was three years old she wanted her doll to be able to walk with her. We measured from where she held her doll's hand to where the doll's feet would touch the ground, and this led to a doll 22 in/56 cm tall.

In addition to my signature rag doll, I've explored a few other sizes. Once I was commissioned to create a 5-ft-10-in/1.8-m "life-size" version of my rag doll. It was such an interesting process to take something that is so delicately detailed and scale it up to something so large. It took me a while to figure it out, but eventually, I just decided to work as though it was small. I used all of the same materials I used in my smaller dolls and gave it the same details. The result was even better than I had envisioned—a very big version of something special.

For this book I have designed a 19-in/48-cm doll with a slightly simplified pattern. I love this new size—it is just right for a first adventure into making a rag doll and is perfect for small arms to hug.

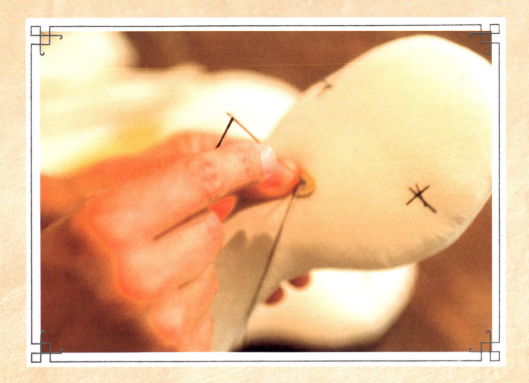

ACCESSORIES

I started making accessories right away. In the beginning, I put so much detail into the original dress the doll was wearing that it would be difficult to remove, so I started creating extra clothing that could be worn over the original outfit. I went antiquing to find doll clothes to use as a basis for my patterns. I was able to find beautiful little capes and coats. Simple aprons and hats were also easy to come by. I used these pieces as inspiration for creating a line of special accessories for the doll.

My favorite doll accessories are simple ones: a shrug, scarf, or coat. I also like to focus on pieces from a certain time period. For instance, I love the style of clothing from the 1920s. There is something so special and sophisticated about that era—the headbands, the fur collars. You can see the influence of the '20s in most of my accessories.

Getting Started

Beginning any new project is exciting, and it's important to consider a number of things before getting started. It's always fun to explore fabrics and notions that can make each project special. This chapter describes where I find inspiration and some of my favorite details. I also discuss the materials, tools, and techniques that will help you make each project a success.

FINDING FABRICS

Before starting any project, I hunt through flea markets and yard sales for fabric that really speaks to me. Shopping in an open-air market is an inspiring and essential part of my process.

Selecting fabric is a tactile experience, through and through. I take into account the workmanship and durability of each piece of fabric I find. Is it soft, strong, beautiful? Will it hold up

in its repurposed life? If the scrap is badly damaged, is there a section that could be used for a doll's apron or as a strip within a small quilt? Visions take shape in my head. If I love a fabric, I will find a way to use it.

There is a story behind everything I pick up. My heart jumps when I come across a piece of raw linen cloth that was clearly meant to be utilitarian, embroidered with just simple initials or flowers, and has been used down to the threads. This type of fabric sparks my creativity: I can imagine making a new object with the cloth so it will be used and loved again in a different incarnation. The idea of designing something from an antique piece of fabric for my everyday modern life is exciting to me.

I love the challenge of figuring out how to use the tattered pieces in my dolls and quilts. Working around someone else's mending, repairs, and darning is a welcome collaboration, and means that each creation will have a history and the potential to become a modern heirloom. The delicate weave of an antique textile shows the craftsmanship of a dying art. There is honesty in fabric.

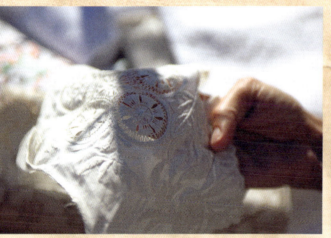

The Making of a Rag Doll

MATERIALS

Choosing and combining beautiful and sustainable materials for each piece is part of creating a true heirloom. My favorite materials are derived from natural sources: repurposed hand-knit sweaters of cashmere and wool and sustainable materials such as corn fiber stuffing and bamboo embroidery floss. I keep in mind that the rag dolls are meant to be held, played with, and loved by children and adults alike, so they should be natural and durable. I am doing my best work when I create something by hand that is both aesthetically beautiful and environmentally responsible.

With today's online access to designers and craftspeople as well as the many shops specializing in natural materials, you can easily source quality materials for making rag dolls and their accessories. (Although I still love nothing more than spending a day wandering through an antique market in search of that one special fabric.) On the pages that follow is a selection of my favorite, sustainable, go-to materials.

✳ ANTIQUE FABRICS AND TRIMS

Working with used fabrics and trims gives each doll a unique quality. Once in a while I come across small bits of lace or velvet ribbon that will work perfectly for ties on doll accessories or for small details in the hair. Generally, I avoid synthetic materials and anything that does not feel good to the touch.

✳ BUTTONS

It is easy to avoid using plastic buttons when shell, wood, and bamboo buttons are so readily available. I especially like the simplicity and feel of an oyster shell button. Small shell buttons work well as detailing for a doll's shoulder where it meets the body. Vintage buttons are wonderful for surprising embellishment on dresses, coats, and shawls. You can find fabulous button collections at thrift shops and flea markets. There are also many online button sources.

✳ CORD

A cord is any string or thin rope that is made up of many strands twisted, braided, or woven together. A thin cotton or bamboo cord works well for the drawstring in a dress or skirt or for the straps on a small linen tote.

✳ EMBROIDERY FLOSS

I prefer embroidery floss in cotton or bamboo, but it is also available in linen, perle, angora, and silk. Embroidery floss is a thread made up of six individual strands that can be separated. You can use any number of strands in the needle, depending on your preferred thread thickness. Embroidery floss is both strong and fade resistant.

Bamboo embroidery floss. Bamboo embroidery floss is perfect for delicate handwork and works well for embroidering the doll faces. It can be a bit hard to find, though. I source mine at my local yarn shop.

Cotton embroidery floss. Cotton embroidery floss is easy to find at any craft store and comes in endless colors. This floss is great for different eye or mouth colors, and because it is machine washable and fade resistant, it is ideal for adding extra details to quilts and clothing.

✳ FABRICS

Whether you love solids, prints, brights, or neutral shades, choosing fabric for each project is very personal. Always choose what speaks to you and go with quality whenever possible. When using a found or repurposed fabric, use your traced patterns to gauge if a piece will be large enough for the project. When buying new fabrics, any standard width will work. Following are some of my favorite fabrics for dolls and accessories.

Cotton muslin, medium weight. I usually work with 100 percent cotton muslin, medium weight, for the body of the rag doll. It has the perfect substance, it's a natural fabric, it's inexpensive, and it's versatile. And a plus: it holds its shape. I look for the coarsest weave because I love seeing the details in the fabric construction. This fabric is soft as soon as it is washed and dried, making it perfect for the finished doll body.

Linen. Linen is a cloth woven from thread made from the fibers of the flax plant. Softened linen is perfect for a doll's dress, while raw, unwashed linen is wonderful for the back of a quilt. The coarse weave in linen is still visible after the fabric has been washed and softened, which gives it textural appeal.

Vintage florals. Floral patterns found on antique fabrics are stunning. I look for antique floral fabrics in cotton, linen, or silk. By merging them into some of my pieces, I hope to further preserve them. I often think, "Am I the last one to see this fabric?"

✳ NATURAL FIBERS

Whenever possible, I use natural fibers that are vegetable or animal in origin. Some of the fibers are from plants; cotton from cotton plants and linen from flax plants. Animal fibers include wool from sheep and silk spun by silkworms.

Cashmere. I am constantly on the lookout for 100 percent cashmere sweaters at flea markets and antique fairs. I repurpose cashmere for use as doll hair. Because it is natural, this fiber tends to get softer and better with age. A cashmere blend also works well, as long as the blend fiber is not synthetic and the texture and quality are good.

Felted wool (laundered, fine-gauge). Sometimes I use strips of wool felt for the doll's hair. You can create a fine felted wool by machine washing and drying any 100 percent wool sweater with heat. I look for sweaters that are thin because as they dry they tend to thicken. And thinner felted wool is easier to cut and sew. Synthetic fibers don't felt well and tend to unravel. Small sheets of felt in a variety of colors can also be found at any craft store.

Yarn. When I am searching for yarns to use for the doll's hair, I look for something really special. A thick, high-quality 100 percent wool yarn works best for making the hair.

✳ PATTERNS

The master pattern for the Jess Brown Rag Doll is provided at the back of the book. You can cut it out, or you can trace or photocopy it and save the pattern for multiple uses. Patterns for a collection of doll accessories are also included in the back of the book.

✳ STUFFING

The stuffing you choose for your doll is a personal choice. There are many natural stuffing options and each type offers different qualities.

Bamboo stuffing. Bamboo stuffing is relatively new to the market. It looks and acts a lot like cotton stuffing. It is eco-friendly and naturally antibacterial.

Corn fiber stuffing. After years of trial and error, I've found that corn fiber stuffing works best for my rag dolls. It is both springy and dense in texture. It feels like an old-world fiber once stuffed into the doll and holds the shape of the doll well.

Cotton stuffing. Cotton fiber is easy to source, but it is less dense than wool or corn fiber so you need to use more to get to a firm feel.

Wool stuffing. Wool stuffing is dense and heavy and creates a firm doll.

✳ THREAD

I care about every stitch that goes into my work, so I choose high-quality threads. I love to be able to see each stitch, so I generally work with dark thread that contrasts with the muslin or linen body fabric. When using my sewing machine to sew a doll's body, I prefer a strong 100 percent cotton/poly all-purpose thread. A blend works best for machine sewing because of its added strength, but for handwork, I generally use a 100 percent cotton or bamboo. I prefer the texture and feel of the cotton and bamboo threads for handwork, and in all cases, black or charcoal gray threads are my go-to colors.

TOOLS

You will need most of the following tools to create the projects in this book, so I suggest keeping them on hand. Your tools do not have to be expensive or technically complicated. A chopstick, some tracing paper, and a soft pencil are very useful tools, and finding your own favorite tools or techniques is all part of the process.

✳ CHOPSTICK

The blunt end of a chopstick is perfect for stuffing a rag doll and turning seamed pieces right-side out. The long, skinny, tapered shape of a chopstick (made from wood, bamboo, ivory, or strong plastic) is just right for pushing stuffing material into long, narrow rag doll arms and legs. You can also use the eraser-end of a pencil.

✳ IRON AND IRONING BOARD

It is helpful to have an iron and a small tabletop ironing board on hand when working on the small doll accessories. You may need to remove wrinkles in fabrics with low heat before pinning and cutting out pattern pieces. And you may need to press pieces as you make them.

✳ NEEDLES

Needles come in many lengths, widths, and shapes depending on their intended use. For instance, different needles work best for beading, embroidering, tatting, and sewing. For soft sculpture like a rag doll, a doll needle is essential. I keep a variety of needles in my studio and have favorites depending on the level of detail needed and the materials I am using.

Doll needle. I use a long (3 to 5 in/7.5 to 12 cm), straight needle commonly called a doll needle when sewing through a stuffed doll's body. This type of needle is also useful for attaching hair and adding facial details to the stuffed doll.

Hand-sewing needles. For hand-sewing, I recommend using needles with a medium eye so you don't create large holes in the fabric. The medium eye easily fits different threads, cords, or floss. It is handy to have an assortment of hand-sewing needles nearby when working with different materials, like lace and buttons. A few projects in the book require a large-eye needle, and this is noted in the instructions.

✳ RULER

A clear, gridded, plastic ruler works best for these projects, because you can lay it directly onto the pattern or fabric and clearly see the measurements as well as what's underneath.

✹ SCISSORS

Scissors, whether for cutting paper or fabric, should be high quality and sized to fit your hand. Make sure to keep your scissors clean and sharpened. Like any tool, scissors should feel right and make your work easier. Always spend a bit more for a quality pair that will last.

Fabric scissors. Fabric scissors have extremely sharp blades for cutting quickly and easily through fabric. Most fabric scissors have stainless-steel blades that make a crisp cut along the entire length of the blade. Save your fabric scissors for just cutting fabric, so the blades don't get dull. Good-quality fabric scissors are a pleasure to use and will last for many years.

Paper scissors. Paper scissors come in a variety of shapes and sizes. They are designed to smoothly cut all types of paper. These scissors generally do not work well on fabric, and if used on anything other than paper, they will dull quickly.

Small scissors. Small, sharp scissors with short, pointed blades are perfect for cutting notches in fabric and when working with fine cotton or bamboo embroidery floss. You don't need to spend a lot on these scissors, but the better the quality, the longer they will last and the better they will perform.

✹ SEAM RIPPER

This tool has a tiny pronged blade at the end for removing a single stitch or a row of stitches. By sliding the blade beneath the stitch and pulling up gently, the stitches are cut but not the fabric. A seam ripper is really handy for quickly removing stitching mistakes.

✳ SEWING MACHINE

There are many options when looking for a sewing machine. Think about what you plan to do with your machine—simple sewing projects or more involved projects such as quilts and upholstery? Chances are a simple sewing machine with a small variety of straight and zigzag stitch options will be perfect as you begin sewing and experimenting with projects. A good used machine is an option.

✳ STRAIGHT PINS

Straight pins are essential for fastening pieces of fabric together and pinning pattern pieces to fabric. I like to use straight pins with rounded colored ends that are easy to see and grip.

✳ TRACING TOOLS

If you choose to trace the patterns, you will need the following tools.

Soft pencil. Soft pencils work well for tracing or marking your fabric. Pencils are graded by the hardness or softness of the graphite used in the pencil. The higher the number, the harder the lead.

Tailor's chalk. I enjoy using tailor's chalk as another option for tracing. This flat, square chalk is traditionally used by tailors to make temporary marks on fabric.

Tracing paper. Tracing paper or vellum work well for tracing the patterns in this book. Trace each piece separately using tracing paper and a soft pencil, and cut out the pieces with your paper scissors. You may also choose to scan or photocopy the pattern pieces.

TERMS AND TECHNIQUES

The projects in this book don't require advanced sewing skills, but you will need to know a few basic terms and techniques. This section will help you brush up on simple techniques before you get started. And you'll find this section a great spot to turn to if you have a question while you're in the middle of a project.

✱ TERMS

I use several sewing terms in the project instructions. If you are new to sewing, I suggest familiarizing yourself with these key terms before getting started.

Baste—to sew using long, loose stitches to hold fabric in place temporarily. Basting can be done by hand or on a sewing machine set to the longest stitch length. Basting stitches are also used for gathering fabric.

Clip—a tiny ($1/8$ in/3 mm) straight snip into the seam allowance, marking an important guide spot on a project. These short cuts can be aligned with other cuts so that your fabric pieces match up well, or they can indicate a fold line or other construction detail.

Grain—the texture created by the threads that run lengthwise and crosswise within a fabric. The grain is parallel with the selvedge edges of the fabric bolt.

Notch—a tiny ($1/8$ in/3 mm) V-shaped cut taken out of the seam allowance on the outside of a curved seam. These small notches help ease out rounded edges and encourage the fabric to lie flat.

Right side (R/S)—the "front" side of the fabric that will face outward when the project is finished; the side of the fabric where the design or pattern is printed.

Seam allowance—the distance between the seam line and the cut edges of the project. For the doll accessory projects in this book, the seam allowance is $1/4$ in/ 6 mm and is built into each pattern piece. It is always a good idea, however, to measure as you go.

Seam line—the sewing line where stitches join two or more pieces of fabric together.

Selvedge—the finished edge of the sides of a woven fabric. The selvedge often has a narrow tape effect that is different from the body of the fabric and easy to identify; on the selvedge edge, the fabric won't fray or unravel. I often use the selvedge edge for visual interest. Some people prefer to trim off the selvedge, because that edge can cause the fabric to shrink and pucker after being laundered. It is not necessary to cut off the selvedge for doll accessories

that will only occasionally be washed. In some of my projects I use the fabric selvedge along a straight edge, eliminating the need for any further finishing on that edge.

Stitch length—the length of each individual stitch. When making rag dolls, stuffing can cause a strain on the seams, so set your machine to a short stitch length to ensure that your seams are strong.

Wrong side (W/S)—the "back" side of the fabric, not the printed side.

✳ TECHNIQUES

This section discusses several skills and activities that are used in the projects, from dyeing fabric to reinforcing seams and hand-stitching. These techniques have worked well for me in my work.

Cutting patterns. Using straight pins, pin the cut pattern pieces to the fabric specified in the project. Trace around each piece with a soft pencil or tailor's chalk and cut along the traced line. You can also skip the tracing step and just pin the pattern piece to the fabric and cut around it. Be careful to keep the pattern piece flat against the fabric to make your cutting as accurate as possible. Use sharp fabric scissors when cutting out fabric pieces.

Some projects call for cutting the pattern pieces "on the fold." This means that you first fold the fabric, right-sides facing, then place the pattern piece right-side up with the edge on the fabric's fold. Read the project instructions carefully as you set up your pattern pieces on the fabric. Pin the pattern piece and the fabric together around the edges. Trace the pattern.

Dyeing fabric. I use black teas to dye the cotton muslin fabric for the doll body. The tea gives softly varied skin tones. To create a black tea dye bath, soak 6 tea bags in a metal tub of hot water until you get a rich brown color. Remove the tea bags and soak the sewn (unstuffed) muslin doll body for at least 3 hours. The soaking time depends on the amount of color you want for your doll: for a darker tone, leave the fabric in the bath longer. Dry flat before stuffing.

Pressing seams open. Using an iron and ironing board, on the wrong side of the fabric, press the seam open until it lies flat. For fragile, thin, or vintage fabrics, place a towel between the fabric and your iron. To avoid burning your fabric, start with a low to medium heat and increase as needed to match the fiber.

Reinforcing seams. Reinforcing seams is an important step in areas that may get extra wear or pressure from stuffing, such as the underarms on a doll. A reinforced seam also keeps the fabric from fraying or unraveling. To reinforce a seam, sew back over the seam line completely or sew back with about six stitches at the beginning and end of the seam.

Seam allowances. All patterns include a $^1/_4$-in/6-mm seam allowance. To easily create this seam line, use the seam allowance marks found on your machine and/or a $^1/_4$-in/6-mm presser foot as your guide.

Sewing curved seams. To sew a curved seam, you need to have control of your fabric as it feeds under the presser foot of your sewing machine. Sew slowly, doing your best to keep the edge of the fabric lined up with the metal seam guide on the bed of your machine beside the needle.

Sewing straight seams. By watching the metal seam guide on the bed of your sewing machine alongside the needle and by keeping the fabric aligned with the guide, you will be able to sew a straight seam. If you watch the sewing machine needle, however, which is constantly moving, it is almost impossible to sew straight. There is no need to sew quickly. Controlling your speed will help you practice sewing a straight seam.

Stitches. Most of the projects in this book are sewn by machine. If you prefer to sew by hand, all projects can be hand-sewn using a small running stitch or whipstitch. Here are my go-to stitches.

Backstitch—to sew about six stitches by machine back over the seam line at the beginning and end of the seam to strengthen the seam ends.

Basting stitch—to sew using the longest stitch length by machine or by hand. Basting is used for making a temporary seam, which can later be removed. Basting is also used for pulling the fabric to make it gather.

Edgestitch—to sew a row of stitches on the wrong side very close ($1/8$ in/3 mm) to a seam line or garment edge in order to hold the pieces firmly in place. Edge-stitching can also be used on the right side of the fabric to add a decorative detail.

Gathering—to create small folds or puckers along the edge of your fabric by sewing two parallel lines using the basting stitch and pulling on the threads to gather the fabric. Some patterns may call for a single line of basting. When basting, do not backstitch at the beginning or end of the stitching line, but do leave long thread tails for gently making the gathers.

Ladder stitch—a commonly used hand-sewing stitch, used to invisibly close openings after stuffing a doll and to join two stuffed parts together. After knotting off, the thread tails can be tucked into the stuffed body.

Staystitch—to sew a line of stitches on a single layer of fabric in order to keep it from stretching or fraying.

Whipstitch—a hand-sewing stitch used to join folded or hemmed edges or to close an opening. Unlike the ladder stitch, this stitch is visible. Slant your needle as you sew to make slanted stitches, or keep the needle upright to make straight stitches.

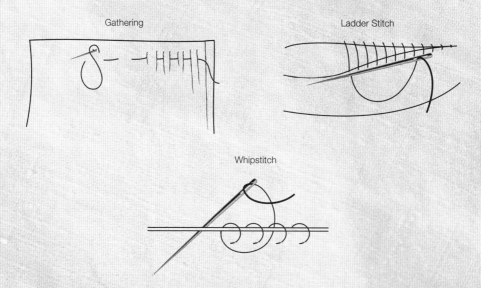

Gathering

Ladder Stitch

Whipstitch

Tracing patterns. To trace a pattern piece, lay tracing paper or vellum over the pattern sheet at the back of the book and trace the lines with a soft pencil or tailor's chalk. Trace each pattern piece separately and as carefully as possible. Be sure to write the name of the project and pattern piece on each traced piece, and transfer any notches or details, such as a pocket placement or grainline.

Pattern Legend	
seam line – – – – – – – – – –	clip mark ⊢
fold line ·–··–··–··–··–··–··	place on fold to cut ↑ ↑
grainline ◄─────────►	

Projects

The Jess Brown Rag Doll

A rag doll becomes personal the moment you begin to cut and sew. The color of the muslin or linen you use, the facial expression, shape of the face, and hairstyle are all ways to make your rag doll your own. Although you will work from the pattern found at the back of the book, get creative with the process. Part of the fun is seeing how each doll evolves as it is sewn and then dressed. Make something lovely!

Materials

Jess Brown Rag Doll Pattern (provided at the back of the book)

$1/2$ yd/46 cm of medium-weight muslin 44 in/112 cm wide in the preferred skin tone, or dyed to the preferred tone

Coordinating thread

1 bag of doll stuffing (your choice)

Tools

Pencil or tailor's chalk

Tracing paper

Paper scissors

Ruler

Straight pins

Fabric scissors

Sewing machine

Small scissors

Iron and ironing board

Chopstick

Hand-sewing needle (medium-eye)

$\longrightarrow$

FOR THE RAG DOLL BODY

1. Trace the Jess Brown Rag Doll Pattern with the pencil and the tracing paper. Using the paper scissors, cut out the traced pattern pieces. The long, narrow arms and legs that are characteristic of the doll require special attention when tracing, cutting, and sewing.

Note: Seam allowances are included in the patterns, but it is essential to cut the pieces out carefully and sew evenly to end up with the correct seam-line shape and seam allowance.

2. Using the ruler, fold over the selvedge edge of the fabric 12 in/30.5 cm toward the center of the fabric, right-sides together, to create a double layer of fabric for the doll Back Body and Leg pattern pieces.

3. Place the three pattern pieces (Front Body, Back Body, and Leg) on the wrong side of the fabric, making sure that the Back Body and Leg pattern pieces are placed on the double layer of fabric. Using straight pins, pin each pattern piece securely in place and trace around the outer edge onto the fabric, using the pencil. Be sure to transfer the Underarm Pivot Points from the Front Body pattern piece onto the fabric. Remove the pattern pieces, repinning the back body and leg pieces to stabilize the double layer of fabric as you cut.

4. Using fabric scissors, cut the fabric along the outside drawn edges. You will end up with five fabric pieces: one front, two backs, and two legs.

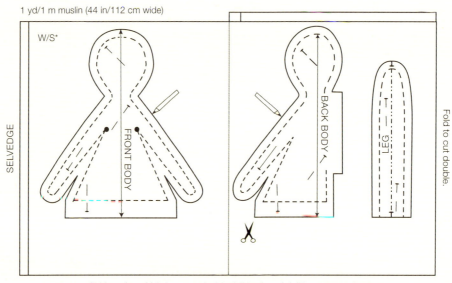

1 yd/1 m muslin (44 in/112 cm wide)

W/S*

SELVEDGE

FRONT BODY

BACK BODY

LEG

Fold to cut double.

Fold portion of fabric to cut double doll back and doll leg pattern pieces.

Steps 2–4

* W/S: wrong side of fabric
  R/S: right side of fabric

5. Pin the two back body pieces, right-sides together, aligning all raw edges.

With the sewing machine, sew the back body pieces together from the top of the head to the top of the center-back opening. Reinforce the beginning and end of the seam with backstitches. Remove the pins.

Sew the back body pieces together from the bottom of the center-back opening to the bottom of the back. Reinforce the beginning of the seam with backstitches. Remove the pins.

6. Using the small scissors, snip about $1/8$ in/3 mm into the seam allowance on the head curve and at the top and bottom of the center-back opening. Be careful not to cut through the stitches of the seam line.

Note: These small snips help create a smoother curve on the head when the doll is turned right-side out and stuffed in the final steps.

7. With the iron set on medium heat, press the snipped, sewn seams open. Use pins to hold the center-back opening together. (Once the doll is sewn, the opening will be used for stuffing the doll.)

$\longrightarrow$

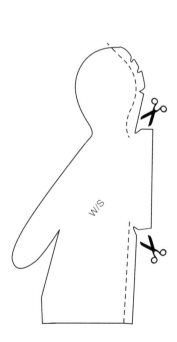

Steps 5-6

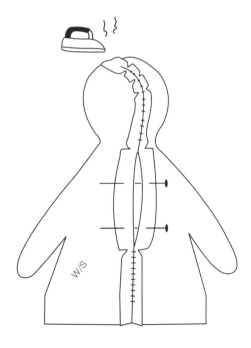

Step 7

8. Pin the front body fabric piece to the back body piece, right-sides together, aligning all raw edges. Sew the pieces together, starting at one bottom corner, going around the top of the body, and ending at the opposite bottom corner, leaving the bottom edge open. When you reach the underarms, sew all the way to the marked Underarm Pivot Points and pivot, with the needle down, before continuing along the outer edge. Reinforce the beginning and end of the seam with backstitches. Be sure to reinforce the underarms after you sew around the body. Sew slowly around the curves, and pivot, with the needle down, when necessary. Remove the pins.

$\longrightarrow$

Step 8

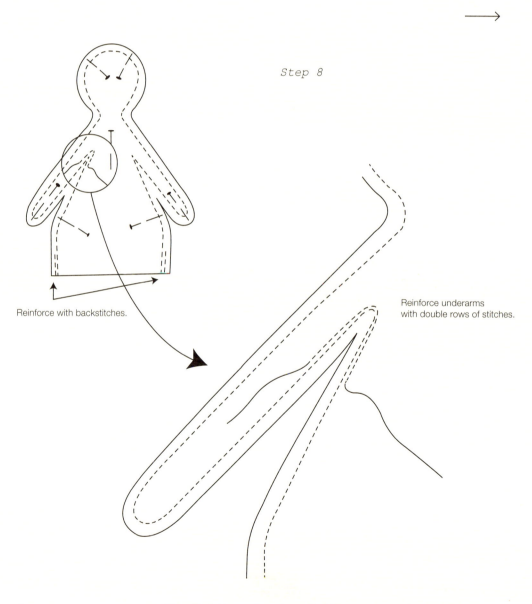

Reinforce with backstitches.

Reinforce underarms with double rows of stitches.

9. Snip ⅛ in/3 mm into all curved seam allowances, to release the tightness of the curved seam. Be careful not to cut through the seam stitches. Clip around the head, the neck, the underarms, and the hands.

10. Turn the body right-side out through the opening at the lower edge. Use the chopstick to turn out the arms. Be patient and gentle.

→

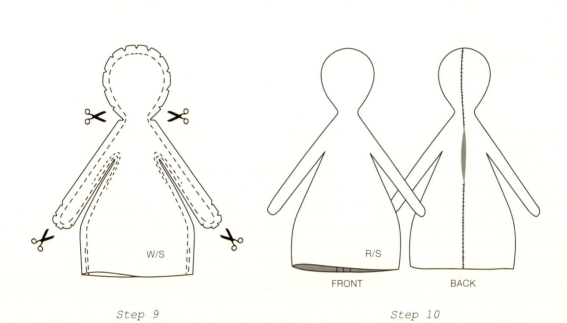

Step 9   Step 10

11. Find the two leg pieces that you cut in step 4. Fold one leg, lengthwise, right-sides together, and pin. Sew the long edges of the leg together. Reinforce the top leg opening and toe points with a few backstitches. Repeat this step for the second leg.

12. Turn both leg pieces right-side out, using the chopstick.

13. Using the stuffing material, stuff both legs until firm. Be patient, and use small pieces of stuffing, one at a time. Leave approximately 1 in/2.5 cm of each leg unstuffed at the open end.

14. Pin the stuffed legs in place at the base of the body between the front and back pieces and roughly 1 in/2.5 cm in from each side of the body.

Note: The stitched seam of each leg is the outer edge seam, so that the doll's toes point inward.

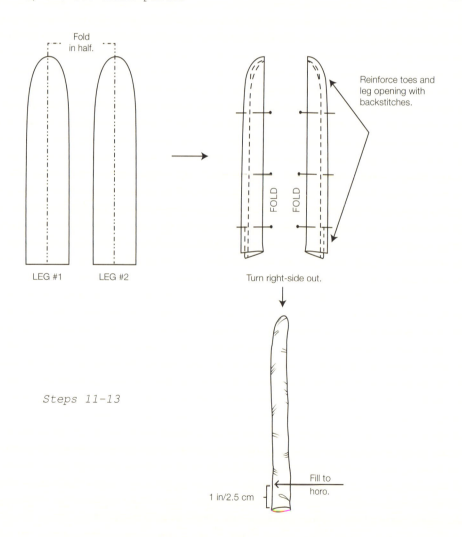

Fold in half.

LEG #1   LEG #2

Steps 11-13

Reinforce toes and leg opening with backstitches.

FOLD   FOLD

Turn right-side out.

Fill to horo.

1 in/2.5 cm

15. Sew a line across the bottom of the body 1 in/2.5 cm up from bottom of the body, to attach the legs and close the bottom of the doll. Remove the pins and reinforce this seam by sewing over it three times. You will have a raw edge where the legs now connect to the body.

16. Stuff the doll body and arms through the vent in the back seam using the chopstick. Work carefully and patiently, using small pieces of stuffing, one at a time. Make sure the doll is evenly stuffed. The doll's neck should not be creased or floppy.

17. Using the hand-sewing needle and thread, hand-stitch the center-back opening closed with two rows of whipstitches.

→

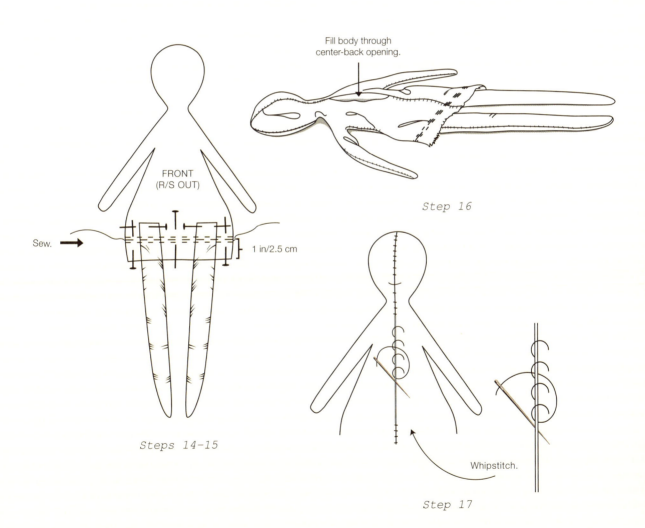

FRONT
(R/S OUT)

Sew. →

1 in/2.5 cm

Steps 14-15

Fill body through center-back opening.

Step 16

Whipstitch.

Step 17

For my rag dolls, I create star-shaped eyes using bamboo embroidery floss, and I make a small heart-shaped mouth using colored felt. These have become characteristic details of my rag dolls, making them personal, unique, and recognizable. Now that you have made your own rag doll, it is time for you to add the final touches. I have some tips and techniques for giving your doll its own expression and personality. Once your doll has its facial features and hair, you can add fun details such as ribbon, pom-poms, buttons, and lace.

✳ FACE

The face you create for your rag doll makes it your own. When made by hand, no two faces are alike.

Materials

Doll needle

Coordinating embroidery floss

Felt

- -
TIPS FOR PERSONALIZING:
- -

Eye and mouth shape, color, and expression are completely up to you. I embroider the eyes and attach the felt mouth using a long doll needle.

For the eyes:

✳ To create the first embroidered star eye, begin by bringing the needle and thread from the back of the doll's head through to the front at point 1 on the diagram below. Stitch down at 2. Come up at 3. Stitch down at 4. Come up at 5 and down at 6 through to the back of the doll's head. Make a secure knot. Repeat this step for the second star eye.

Star Stitch

For the mouth:

* I prefer to cut a freehand heart shape out of felt—this makes every doll a little different. I attach the felt mouth using a long doll needle and embroidery floss.

I bring the needle and thread from the back of the doll's head through to the front and back again, and finish by knotting the embroidery floss at the back of the head. All knots and stitches on the back of the head are eventually covered by the doll's hair.

✳ HAIR

The hair is another fun way to give your rag doll a distinct personality. The material you choose for the hair and how you choose to style it will change the look of your doll. A doll with braided yarn or pigtails has a more playful and childlike look, while a short bob in cashmere is more sophisticated. Have fun with this final and very important detail!

Materials

Felted wool, or printed fabric scraps, yarn, or cord

Coordinating embroidery floss

Doll needle

TIPS FOR PERSONALIZING:

The color and texture of the hair will give your doll a unique look. Yarn, printed fabrics, or felted wools each create a completely different look and can be trimmed to any desired length.

For the hair:

* To create the hair, cut felted wool or printed fabric scraps into strips approximately $1^1/_2$ in/4 cm wide by 12 in/ 30.5 cm long. I use a whipstitch to attach the strips in rows to the rag doll's head. I love using dark embroidery floss that sometimes blends and sometimes contrasts with the color(s) of the felt, yarn, or fabric. Keep in mind that yarn or cord can be braided or tied into pigtails for a playful look for your doll.

Knickers

✳

Every rag doll needs a pair of knickers. These bloomers look adorable as a layer beneath the sundress, drawstring dress, or with any combination of accessories. Once you are comfortable with this pattern, you can easily adjust the length to suit the season.

Materials

Knickers Pattern (provided at the back of the book)

$1/4$ yd/23 cm of solid linen or cotton print fabric

Coordinating thread

Coordinating embroidery floss

Tools

Pencil or tailor's chalk

Tracing paper

Paper scissors

Straight pins

Fabric scissors

Sewing machine

Iron and ironing board

Small scissors

Hand-sewing needle (large-eye)

$\longrightarrow$

1. Using the pencil and tracing paper, trace the Knickers
Pattern.

2. Using the paper scissors, cut
out the Knickers pattern piece.

3. Fold the fabric in half,
right-sides together, to create
a double layer of fabric.

4. Place the Knickers pattern
piece on the folded fabric with
the waist edge on the selvedge
edge. Using the straight pins,

pin the pattern securely in
place and trace around all
outer edges using the pencil.
If you choose not to use the
selvedge edge, you can staystitch the raw waist edge.
Unpin the pattern piece.

5. Pin the layers together and
cut out the knickers using fabric scissors.

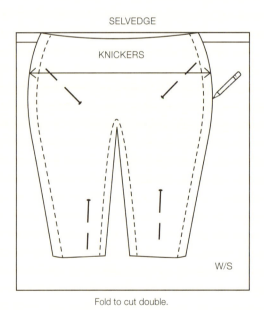

Fold to cut double.

Step 4

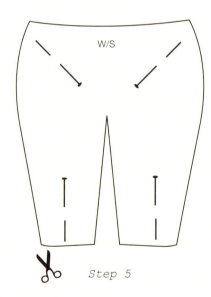

Step 5

The Making of a Rag Doll

6. With the sewing machine, sew the side seams of the knickers. Reinforce the beginning and end of each seam with backstitches.

7. With the iron set on medium heat, press the seam open at the hemline of the knickers only.

8. Turn the knickers right-side out and sew a zigzag stitch line around the knickers hemline to staystitch (both legs). Turn the knickers wrong-side out and pin the inside leg seam.

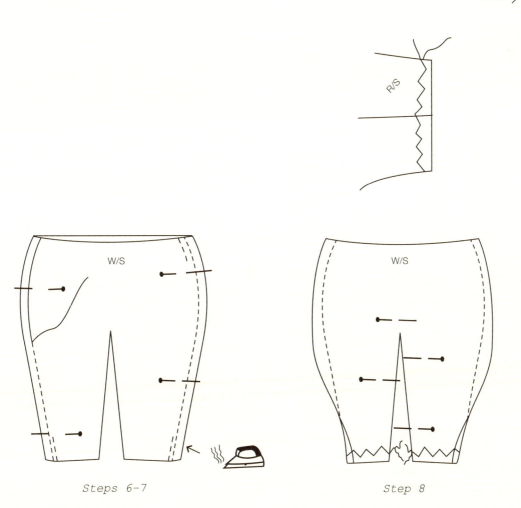

Steps 6-7

Step 8

9. Sew the inside leg seam.
Reinforce the beginning and end
of the seam with backstitches.
Also reinforce the crotch area.
Sew slowly around the curves,
and pivot, with the needle down,
when necessary. Remove the pins.

10. With the small scissors,
snip between the legs in a
Y shape to ease the curve. Cut
just to the stitch line, being
careful not to cut through the
stitches. This cut will ease
the fabric around the curve.

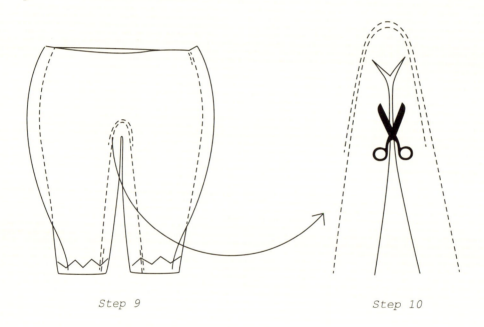

Step 9   Step 10

The Making of a Rag Doll

11. Turn the knickers right-side out. Thread the hand-sewing needle with embroidery floss (using 4 to 6 strands of the floss will work well). Sew running stitches approximately ¼ in/6 mm from the waistline, starting at the center front waist around the waistline and back again, to make a drawstring waist. Make sure to leave enough floss length so that you can easily dress the doll, tighten the drawstring waist, and tie a bow. Then knot each end of the drawstring to keep the ends from slipping back through the holes.

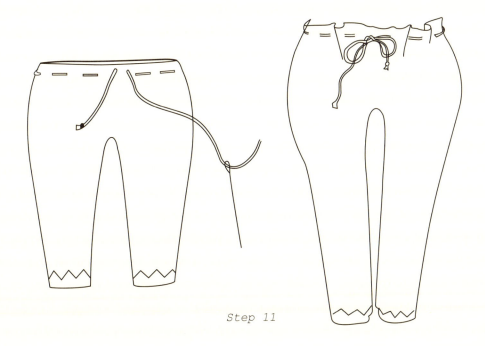

Step 11

Newspaper Hat

✳

Create a classic newspaper hat for your doll to wear around the house or out on adventures. You can substitute newspaper with vintage wrapping paper, old book pages, or pages from magazines for endless different looks. Finish the edges by hand or with the zigzag stitch setting on your sewing machine. Add a pom-pom or a feather as the perfect finishing touch.

Materials

1 sheet of newspaper

Coordinating 100 percent cotton/poly all-purpose thread, for a zigzag finished edge

Coordinating embroidery floss, for a tassel

Yarn (any color), for a pom-pom

Feather

Clear-drying paper glue, for a feather

Tools

Pencil

Ruler

Paper scissors

Sewing machine, for a zigzag finished edge

Small scissors and hand-sewing needle (medium-eye), for a tassel or a pom-pom

⟶

1. Using the pencil and ruler, draw a 7 1/2-by-9 5/8-in/19-by 24.5-cm rectangle on the newspaper. Cut out the rectangle with paper scissors.

Note: Vintage wrapping paper or double-sided decorative paper sheets also make great hats.

2. Crease the center of the cut rectangle vertically and then horizontally.

3. Fold in half along the horizontal crease.

4. Fold the top corners down to touch the center crease. Leave a 1/8-in/3-mm gap on each side of the crease at the top.

5. Fold the bottom flap up over the bottom of the triangle folds. Turn the hat to the opposite side and fold the bottom edge up to match.

6. Open the hat at the bottom edge and shape it to fit your doll's head.

→

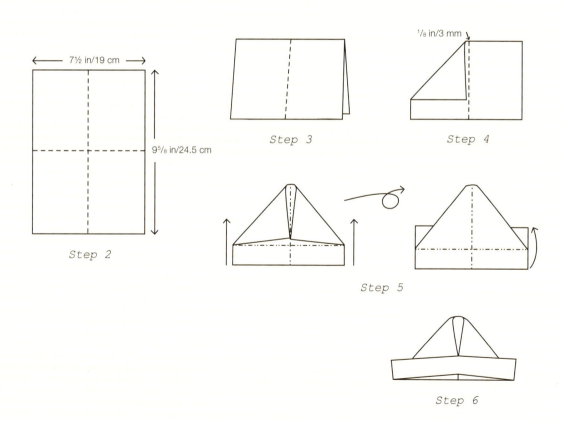

← 7½ in/19 cm →

9⅝ in/24.5 cm

Step 2

Step 3

1/8 in/3 mm

Step 4

Step 5

Step 6

The Making of a Rag Doll

7. Choose your final touches:

For a zigzag finished edge:

* You can use your sewing machine on the zigzag setting to add detail along the front and back edges of the newspaper hat.

For a tassel:

* Cut a piece of embroidery floss 20 in/50 cm long.

* Wrap the floss around two fingers, making a small loop. Remove the loop from your fingers.

* Tie a tight knot at the lower half of the loop.

* Using the small scissors, cut through the upper half of the loop.

* Using the hand-sewing needle and the embroidery floss, stitch the tassel to the upper right side of the hat.

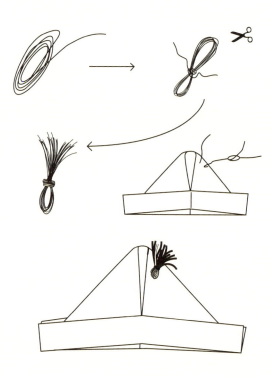

The Making of a Rag Doll

For a pom-pom:

* Cut a piece of yarn 30 in/
  76 cm long.

* Wrap the yarn around two
  fingers, making a small loop.
  Remove the loop from your
  fingers.

* Tie a tight knot around the
  center of the loop.

* Leave a tail of yarn about
  2 in/5 cm long for later
  attaching the pom-pom to
  the hat.

* Using the small scissors, cut
  through the upper and lower
  loops. Spread out the yarn
  and trim to create a rounded
  pom-pom shape.

* Thread the hand-sewing needle
  with the yarn tail on the
  pom-pom.

* Stitch the pom-pom to the
  upper right side of the hat
  by sewing through the newspaper. Make a small knot on
  the inside of the hat to
  hold the pom-pom in place.

For a feather:

* Attach the feather to your
  hat with a dot of the clear-
  drying paper glue.

Sundress

✸

This sundress will inspire you to make all the accessories for your rag doll. To create a collection of garments and accessories, choose fabrics that speak to you (vintage or new, floral, stripe, or solid) and make a few at a time so your doll has options. The sundress is lovely on its own, worn over the knickers, or worn with an apron or coat.

Materials

Sundress Pattern (provided at the back of the book)

¼ yd/23 cm of linen or cotton fabric

Coordinating thread

2 pieces of ribbon or cord, each 4½ in/11 cm long

Tools

Pencil or tailor's chalk

Tracing paper

Paper scissors

Straight pins

Fabric scissors

Sewing machine

Iron and ironing board

Hand-sewing needle (large-eye)

$\longrightarrow$

1. Using the pencil and the tracing paper, trace the Sundress Pattern.

2. Using the paper scissors, cut out the Sundress pattern piece.

3. Place the Sundress pattern piece on the wrong side of the fabric. Using straight pins, pin the pattern securely in place and trace around all outer edges using a pencil. Remove the pattern and the pins. Mark the fold line and tie-strap markers on the right side of the fabric.

4. Using the fabric scissors, cut out the sundress.

$\longrightarrow$

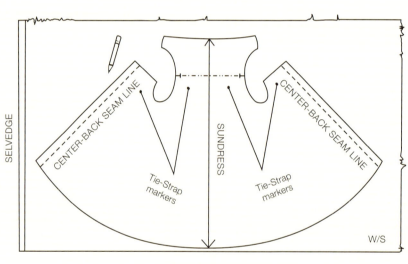

Step 3

5. Using the sewing machine and a medium-length stitch, sew a line $^{1}/_{4}$ in/6 mm from the bottom edge (hemline) to staystitch the edge.

6. Fold down the top portion of the sundress (the neck piece) and pin it securely using straight pins. Sew a line $^{1}/_{4}$ in/6 mm from the bottom raw edge of the folded-down neck piece. Next, sew a line $^{1}/_{8}$ to $^{1}/_{4}$ in/3 to 6 mm from the

edge around the entire top of the sundress including the armhole edges and the folded-down neck piece.

7. With right-sides together, pin and sew the center-back seam. Reinforce the beginning and end of the seam with back-stitches. With the iron set on medium heat, press the seam open.

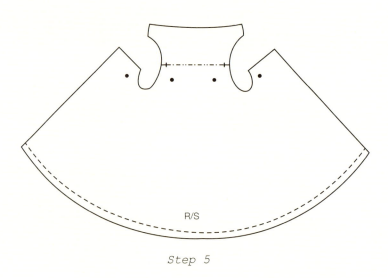

R/S

Step 5

8. Turn the sundress right-side out.

Cut the two pieces of ribbon in half. Knot one end of each of the ribbon pieces. Using the large-eyed hand-sewing needle, thread each of the 2 1/4-in-/6-cm-long pieces from the outside to the inside at the tie-strap markers to create four tie-strap ends. Tie the ends over the doll's shoulders.

Note: *Because of the size of the doll's head, I find it works best to dress the rag doll legs-first. It often requires some squeezing of the legs and hips to put on the clothing, but it's good to avoid squeezing the doll's head if possible.*

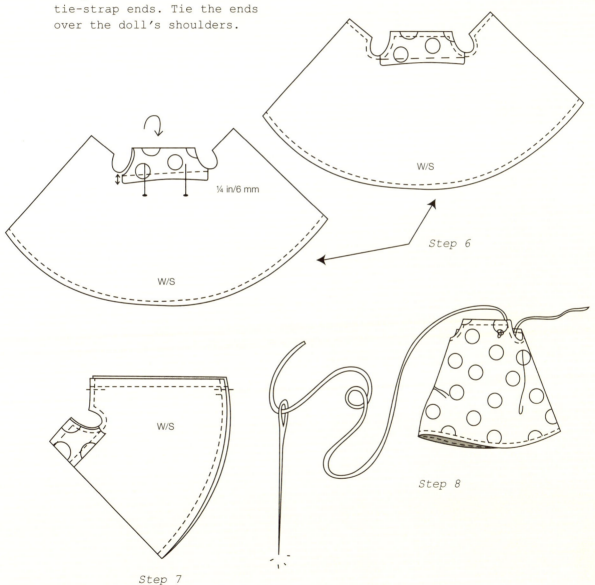

¼ in/6 mm

W/S

W/S

Step 6

W/S

Step 7

Step 8

Tote Bag

✳

A stylish tote is the perfect accessory for your rag doll. It's great for carrying a mini crossword puzzle or tiny handmade book. The project is designed to give you the opportunity to play with small swatches of fabric for a truly original result. I love the shape and details in this tote bag.

Materials

Tote Bag Pattern (provided at the back of the book)

$1/4$ yd/23 cm of solid linen or cotton print fabric, for tote bag body

1 by 10 in/2.5 by 25 cm of matching or contrasting fabric, for tote bag strap

Coordinating thread

Coordinating embroidery floss

Tools

Pencil or tailor's chalk

Tracing paper

Paper scissors

Straight pins

Ruler

Fabric scissors

Small scissors

Sewing machine

Hand-sewing needle

$\longrightarrow$

1. Using the pencil and the tracing paper, trace the two Tote Bag pattern pieces (the Tote Bag and the Tote Bag Strap).

2. Cut out the two pattern pieces using the paper scissors.

3. Place the pattern pieces on the wrong side of the fabric. Using the straight pins, pin the pattern pieces in place.

Trace around all edges, using the pencil. Be sure to transfer the location of notches for fold lines to the seam allowance. Remove the paper pattern pieces and the pins.

4. With the fabric scissors, cut out the tote bag pieces. With the small scissors, snip the fold-line notches where indicated, no more than $1/8$ in/3 mm deep.

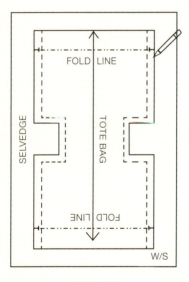

Step 3

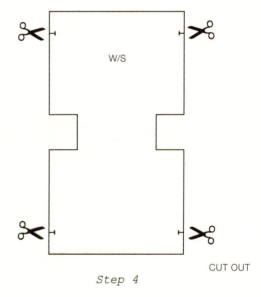

Step 4

CUT OUT

5. Turn the fabric right-side up. Fold the flaps at each end to the right side along the fold lines, and edgestitch the raw edge in place.

6. Fold the tote bag piece in half, right-sides together. With straight pins, pin the two side seams together. Using the sewing machine, sew the side seams, reinforcing both seams at the

top and bottom with backstitches, especially at the upper edge opening down the side of the flaps.

7. Push the bottom of the tote bag up and fold the sides in, aligning the edges of the bottom with the lower edges of the sides so you create a boxy shape. Sew the seams at each side.

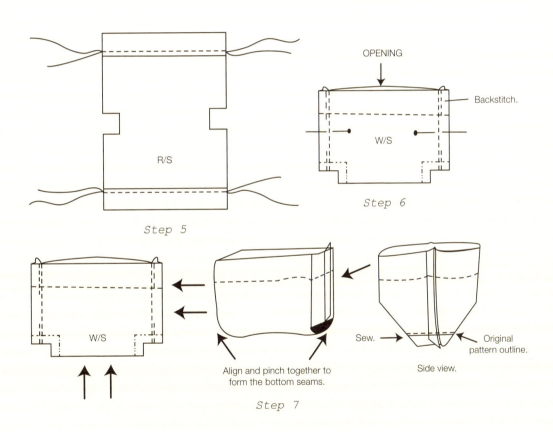

Step 5

Step 6

OPENING

Backstitch.

W/S

Align and pinch together to form the bottom seams.

Sew.

Original pattern outline.

Side view.

Step 7

8. Resew both of these seams to reinforce the ends, completing the bottom of the tote bag. Turn the tote bag right-side out.

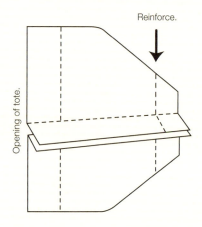

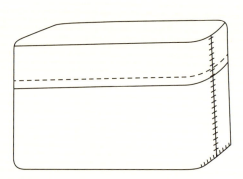

Three-quarter view of Tote Bag turned right-side out.

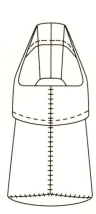

Side view of Tote Bag showing details.

Step 8

The Making of a Rag Doll

9. Fold the strap fabric piece in half lengthwise, wrong-sides together. Down the right side of the fabric on the long edge, edgestitch the folded piece together.

10. Attach the strap to the tote bag at the side seams, using a hand-sewing needle and the embroidery floss to sew embroidery cross-stitches with straight stitches above and below.

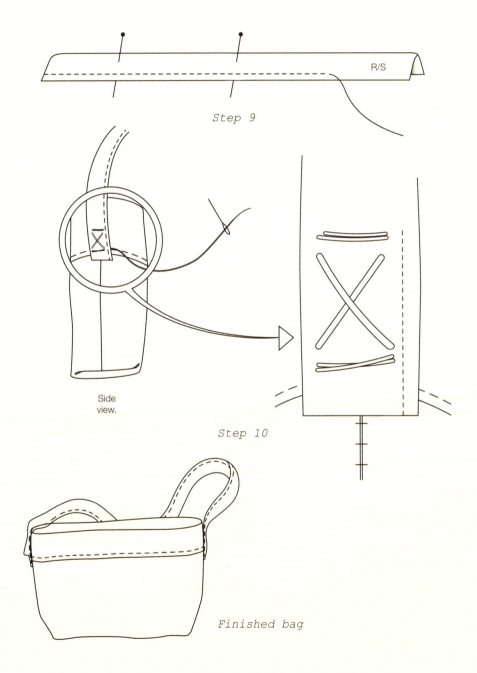

Step 9

Side view.

Step 10

Finished bag

Overcoat

✳

This coat is a variation of the travel coat that I offer as part of my doll accessory collection. Sewn in linen or cotton fabric, it is designed to layer perfectly over the other garment pieces. The drawstring at the neck is an attractive detail that, when tied, helps the coat stay put.

Materials

Overcoat Pattern (provided at the back of the book)

$1/4$ yd/23 cm of solid linen or cotton fabric

Coordinating thread

1 piece of ribbon or cord, 8 in/20 cm long

Tools

Pencil or tailor's chalk

Tracing paper

Paper scissors

Straight pins

Fabric scissors

Sewing machine

Small scissors

Iron and ironing board

Hand-sewing needle (large-eye)

$\longrightarrow$

1. Using the pencil and tracing paper, trace the Overcoat Back and Overcoat Front Patterns.

2. Using the paper scissors, cut out the traced Overcoat Back and Front pattern pieces.

3. Fold the fabric selvedge-edge to selvedge-edge to create a double layer of fabric for the Overcoat Front pattern piece (if you are using raw edges, staystitch a line about ¼ in/ 6 mm from each raw edge before cutting). Place the Front pattern piece on the double layer of fabric. Using straight pins, pin the pattern piece in place. Using the pencil, trace around all outer edges and mark the fold line. Remove the pattern piece, repinning the double layer of fabric to stabilize it as you cut. Using the fabric scissors, cut the fabric along the outside drawn edges.

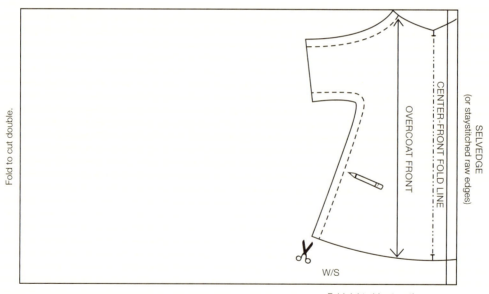

Fold right-sides together
to cut double (Overcoat Front).

Step 3

The Making of a Rag Doll

4. Unfold the remaining fabric and pin the Overcoat Back pattern piece to it. Trace the outer edges, then remove the pattern piece and pins and cut around the drawn edges with fabric scissors.

5. Fold the edges of the two coat front pieces onto the right side of the fabric along the fold line, and use the sewing machine to edgestitch into place. Reinforce the beginning and end of the edgestitch line with backstitches. Trim away the thread tails.

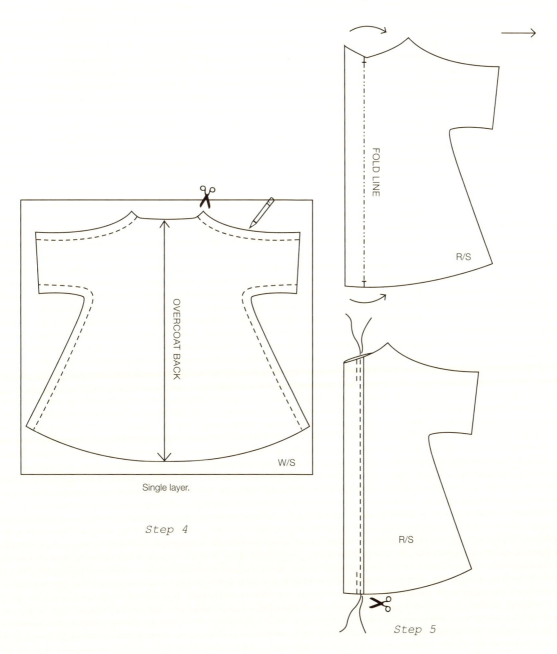

Single layer.

Step 4

Step 5

6. Place the coat front and back pieces together, right-sides facing, and pin the shoulder seams together. Using the sewing machine, sew the shoulder seams and reinforce the seam with backstitches at the neckline and the cuff. Using the small scissors, cut notches to ease the shoulder curve, being very careful not to cut into the stitch line.

7. With the iron set on medium heat, press the shoulder seams open. Staystitch around the edge of the cuff, $1/4$ in/6 mm in from the edge.

8. Pin, then sew the two side seams. Reinforce the beginning and end of the seams with back-stitches.

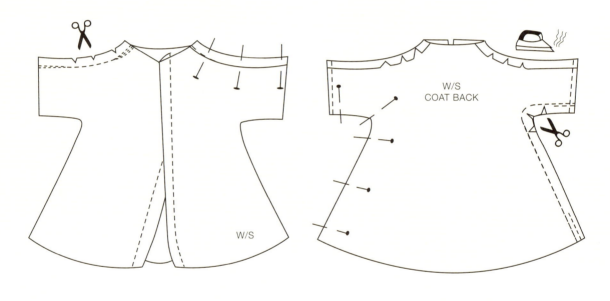

Step 6   *Steps 7–9*

The Making of a Rag Doll

9. Using the small scissors, clip notches into the curved seam allowances at the under-arms, being careful not to cut into the stitch line.

10. Turn the coat right-side out and staystitch the hemline 1/4 in/6 mm from the lower edge.

11. Thread the large-eyed hand-sewing needle with the piece of ribbon, and using running stitches, sew around the neck about 1/4 in/6 mm from the edge to make a drawstring closure. Knot the ends of the ribbon for the final touch.

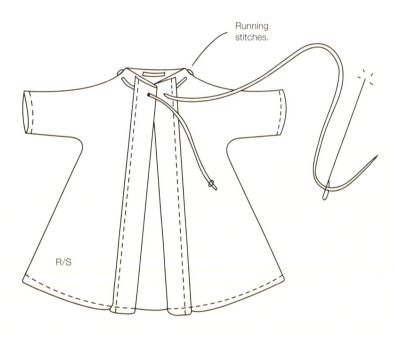

Running stitches.

R/S

Steps 10-11

Quilt

A custom quilt in any size allows you to play with combinations of your favorite fabric scraps. I love combining a neutral palette of raw, white, or gray linen with small sections of bright floral prints. When you work with scraps, each quilt you make will be unique and tell a story. Once you have mastered the doll-size quilt, the instructions easily adapt to crib and throw size—just alter the measurements based on your desired finished dimensions.

Materials

5 fabric scraps in assorted solids and prints, each measuring at least 4 by 18 in/ 10 by 46 cm

Coordinating thread

$1/2$ yd/0.5 m of medium-weight solid cotton or linen for backing fabric

Tools

Pencil or tailor's chalk

Ruler

Fabric scissors

Straight pins

Sewing machine

Seam ripper

Iron and ironing board

Small scissors

$\longrightarrow$

1. Using the pencil and ruler, draw a 3-by-17-in/7.5-by-43-cm rectangle on each of your five fabric scraps. Cut out each rectangle with the fabric scissors. I have named the strips A, B, C, D, and E for your reference in the illustrations.

2. Starting with strips A and B, place the two strips together, right-sides facing, and pin together along one long edge. Then pin strip C to B, right-sides together, along one long edge. Repeat with remaining strips until all five are pinned together along the long edges.

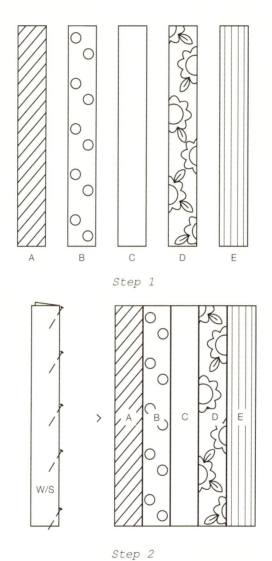

Step 1

Step 2

The Making of a Rag Doll

3. Set your sewing machine to the longest stitch for basting the pieces together. Sew the pinned strips together on the long edges, wrong-side up. Do not backstitch. Remove the pins.

4. With right-sides together, pin together, then sew the long cut edge of strip A to strip E, using a ½-in/12-mm seam allowance. All the strips are now joined into a tube, wrong-sides facing out.

$\longrightarrow$

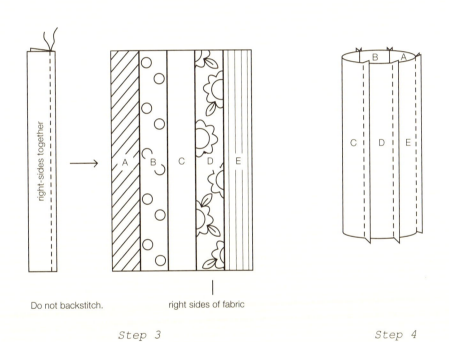

Do not backstitch. right sides of fabric

Step 3   *Step 4*

5. Flatten the tube so that the seam for strips A and E is on an edge.

6. Measure down from the top of the tube and cut across the tube at 3-in/7.5-cm increments three times and a 4-in/10-cm increment once. You will have three 3-in/7.5-cm-tall loops and two 4-in/10-cm-tall loops.

$\longrightarrow$

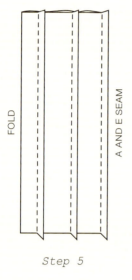

FOLD

A AND E SEAM

Step 5

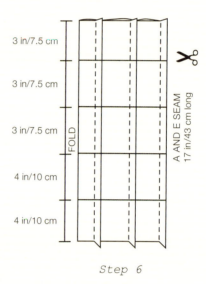

3 in/7.5 cm

3 in/7.5 cm

3 in/7.5 cm

4 in/10 cm

4 in/10 cm

FOLD

A AND E SEAM
17 in/43 cm long

Step 6

The Making of a Rag Doll

7. Using the seam ripper, take one loop and open the A/E seam carefully. The basting stitches should come out easily. Repeat, as follows, to open the remaining four loops:

* Open the A/B seam on the second loop.

* Open the B/C seam on the third loop.

* Open the C/D seam on the fourth loop.

* Open the D/E seam on the fifth loop.

You will now have five strips of assorted fabrics. Press the seams open using an iron on medium heat.

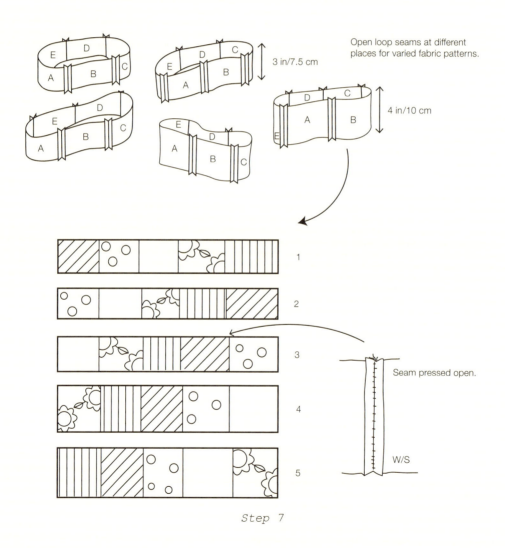

Open loop seams at different places for varied fabric patterns.

3 in/7.5 cm

4 in/10 cm

Seam pressed open.

W/S

Step 7

The Making of a Rag Doll

8. Arrange the strips in any order you like to make the quilt top. Change the stitch length on your sewing machine to medium. Pin two strips together along the long sides, right-sides facing, and sew them together with a $^1/_2$-in/12-mm seam allowance. Repeat with the remaining strips to complete the quilt top. Using an iron on medium heat, press open all newly sewn seams and edgestitch on both sides of each horizontal seam.

$\longrightarrow$

A	B	C	D	E
E	A	B	C	D
D	E	A	B	C
C	D	E	A	B
B	C	D	E	A

Sew strips with right-sides together to make quilt top.

Step 8

9. Using the pencil and ruler, draw a 12-by-26-in/30.5-by-66-cm rectangle on your backing fabric and cut out the rectangle with the fabric scissors. Fold the backing fabric in half, wrong-sides facing, so you end up with a double piece of backing fabric that measures 12 by 13 in/30.5 by 33 cm.

Center the quilt top on the backing fabric, wrong-side down. Smooth out all the layers well and pin the quilt top to the backing fabric. Trim all the layers so that the edges are even and the quilt measures 12 by 13 in/30.5 by 33 cm. Use the stitch-in-the-ditch technique to sew the quilt top and backing together, starting in the middle of the quilt and working out toward the edges.

Note: To stitch-in-the-ditch, simply keep the stitch line as close to the seam as possible. This technique will anchor the key seam lines in your quilt and the stitches will be nearly invisible.

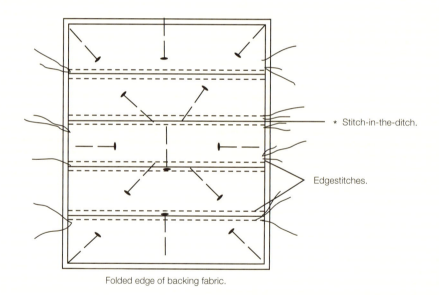

* Stitch-in-the-ditch.

Edgestitches.

Folded edge of backing fabric.

Step 9

10. With the iron set on medium heat, press your quilt.

11. Sew the outside edge of the quilt top to the backing fabric ½ in/12 mm from the quilt top's edge, around all four sides.

12. With the small scissors, create a fringed edge by making tiny straight cuts into the backing fabric ¼ in/6 mm apart. Fringe all four sides of the quilt. Go slowly and be careful not to cut into the stitches.

Steps 10-11

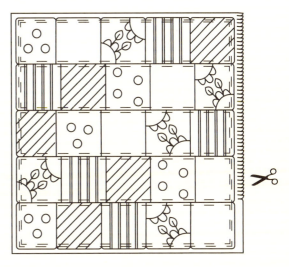

Step 12

Drawstring Dress

✳

This dress is perfect for your rag doll when the occasion calls
for more than a sundress. The design is classic and invites
variation—once you have made one, you may choose to shorten the
pattern to make a tunic to be worn over the knickers or as a cute
layer over the sundress. Adjust the sleeve length as desired and
add sweet details such as the drawstring tie at the neckline.

Materials

Drawstring Dress Pattern
(provided at the back of
the book)

$1/4$ yd/23 cm of linen or
cotton fabric

2 pieces of embroidery floss or
cord, each $4^1/_2$ in/11 cm long

Coordinating thread

Tiny button

Tools

Pencil or tailor's chalk

Tracing paper

Paper scissors

Straight pins

Fabric scissors

Small scissors

Sewing machine

Iron and ironing board

Hand-sewing needle
(medium-eye)

$\longrightarrow$

1. Using the pencil and tracing paper, trace the two Drawstring Dress pattern pieces (Front and Back).

2. Using the paper scissors, cut out the two pattern pieces.

3. Fold one edge of the fabric 10 in/25 cm in toward the center, right-sides facing and wrong-side up, to create a double layer of fabric for the Drawstring Dress Back pattern piece. Place the Drawstring Dress Front on the single layer of fabric and the Drawstring Dress Back on the double layer of fabric. Using straight pins, pin each pattern piece securely in place and trace all outer edges using the pencil. Make sure to transfer the mark for the back neck opening. Remove the pattern pieces, repinning the dress back to stabilize the double layer of fabric as you cut.

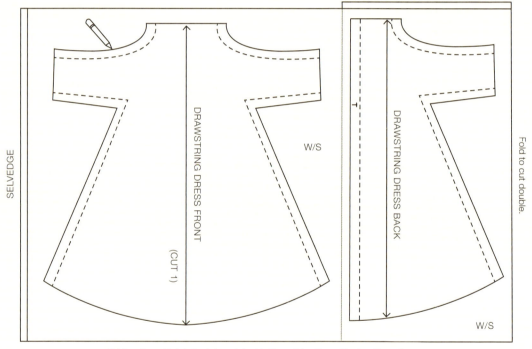

Fold portion of fabric back to cut double Drawstring Dress Front pattern pieces.

Step 3

The Making of a Rag Doll

4. Using the fabric scissors, cut out the front piece and the two back pieces (one back piece is the reverse image of the other). With the small scissors, snip a $1/8$-in/3-mm notch in the seam allowance at your pencil mark to mark the back neck opening.

$\longrightarrow$

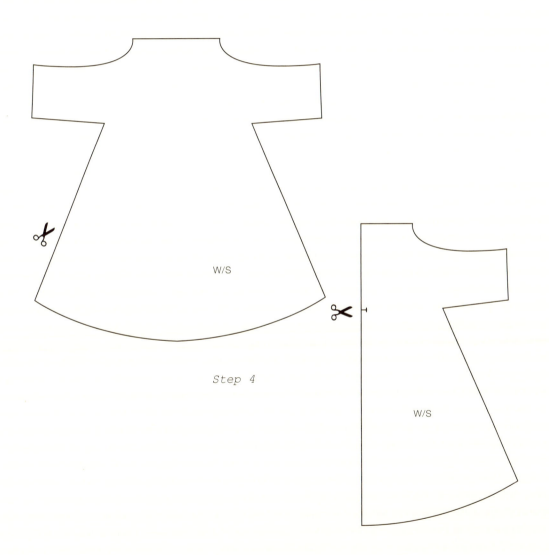

Step 4

5. Using the sewing machine and starting at the back neck opening notch, sew the back pieces together, right-sides facing, along the center back seam. Reinforce the beginning and end of the seam with backstitches. With the iron set on medium heat, press the seam open, including the seam allowance above the notch.

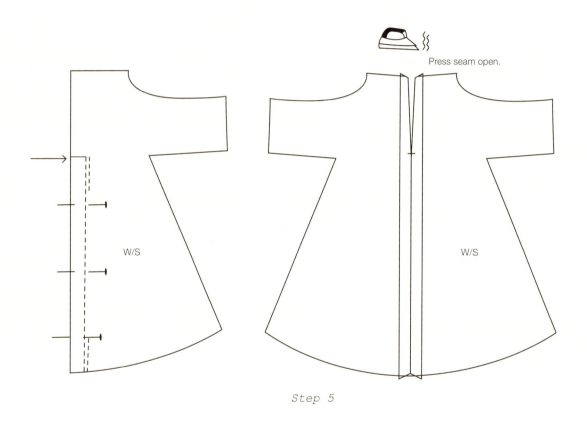

Press seam open.

W/S

W/S

Step 5

6. Edgestitch the two sides of the back neckline opening ⅛ in/ 3 mm in from the edge.

7. Pin the front and back shoulders together, right-sides facing. Using the sewing machine, sew the shoulder seams, reinforcing the beginning and end of the seam with backstitches.

8. With the small scissors, clip notches into the seam allowance for both shoulder seams to ease the curve, being careful not to cut into the seam stitches. Press the seam open.

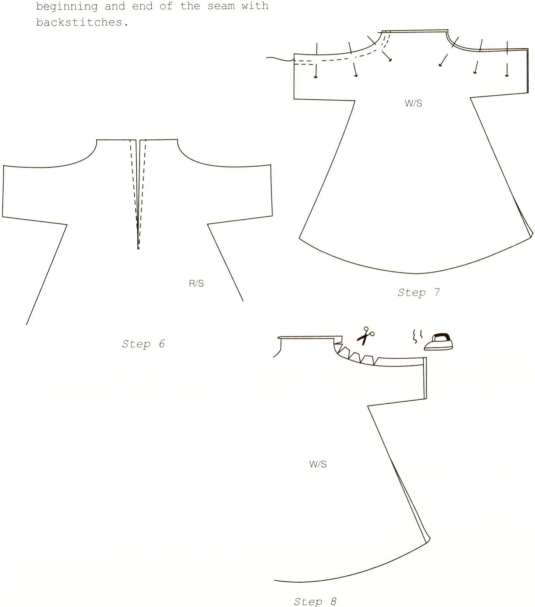

Step 6

Step 7

Step 8

9. Turn up the cuff to the wrong side and edgestitch in place along the raw edge, with the flat shoulder seam under the cuff edge.

10. Pin the side and bottom sleeve seams together, right-sides facing. Beginning at the cuff edge, sew the sleeve seam. Pivot at the underarm and sew the side seam, reinforcing the seam at the beginning and the end with backstitches.

11. Reinforce the underarm seam with a second row of machine stitches on top of the first stitched line. With the small scissors, clip into the seam allowance to ease the underarm, being careful not to cut into the stitches. Press the seams open.

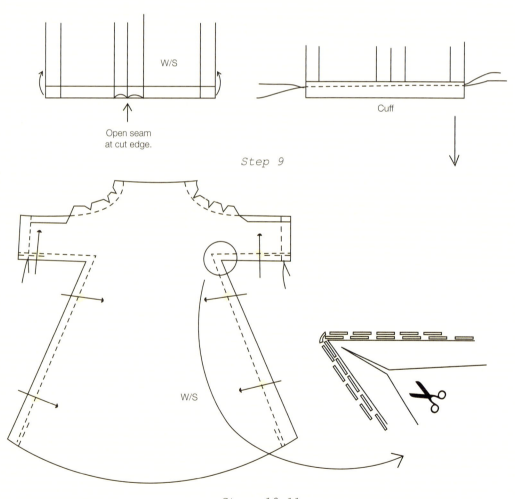

W/S

Open seam
at cut edge.

Cuff

Step 9

W/S

Steps 10–11

The Making of a Rag Doll

12. Turn the dress right-side out. Staystitch the hemline ¹/₄ in/6 mm from the edge of the dress.

With one of the pieces of embroidery floss, thread the hand-sewing needle.

13. Place a pin to mark the center front. Beginning at one side of the center back, work a running stitch, ¹/₄ in/6 mm from the raw edge of the neck around to the center front. Repeat with the other piece of embroidery floss for the other side. Thread the tiny button on the center front floss tails. Double-knot the floss tails and tie in a bow. To finish off the back tails, tie a small double-knot at the end of each tail.

Steps 12-13   Step 14

Sweater Scrap Hat

❋

You can transform a favorite old sweater into a soft hat to coordinate with the rest of your doll's growing collection of accessories. Then, just cut a thin strip of the same sweater or a favorite scrap of solid or printed fabric to make a complementary scarf.

Materials

Sweater Scrap Hat Pattern (provided at the back of the book)

2 pieces of laundered (felted), fine-gauge knitted wool, at least 5$\frac{1}{2}$ by 4$\frac{1}{2}$ in/14 by 11 cm

Coordinating thread

Scrap of favorite solid or printed fabric, about 6$\frac{1}{2}$ by 1 in/16.5 by 2.5 cm

Tools

Pencil or tailor's chalk

Ruler

Fabric scissors

Tracing paper

Paper scissors

Straight pins

Sewing machine

Small scissors

$\longrightarrow$

1. Using the pencil and ruler, measure two $5^1/_2$-by-$4^1/_2$-in/ 14-by-11-cm pieces of laundered (felted), fine-gauge knitted wool. Cut them out with fabric scissors. Place the pieces together, right-sides facing.

2. With the pencil and tracing paper, trace the two Sweater Scrap Hat Patterns (the Hat and Hat Bow). Cut out the pattern pieces with the paper scissors.

Lay the Hat pattern piece on the stacked wool rectangles, leaving $^3/_8$ in/1 cm at both bottom corners. Pin down the pattern piece and draw around it with the pencil. Remove the pattern piece, repinning the stacked rectangles to stabilize the fabric as you sew.

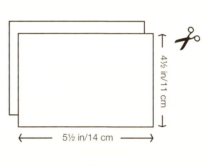

Step 1

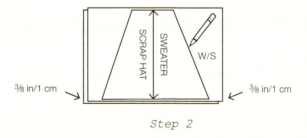

Step 2

3. Using the sewing machine, sew along the drawn diagonal lines of the hat seams and reinforce the beginning and ends of the seams with backstitches.

4. With the fabric scissors, cut away the excess wool fabric, leaving a ¹/₄-in/6-mm seam allowance beyond the seam stitch lines. Turn the hat right-side out.

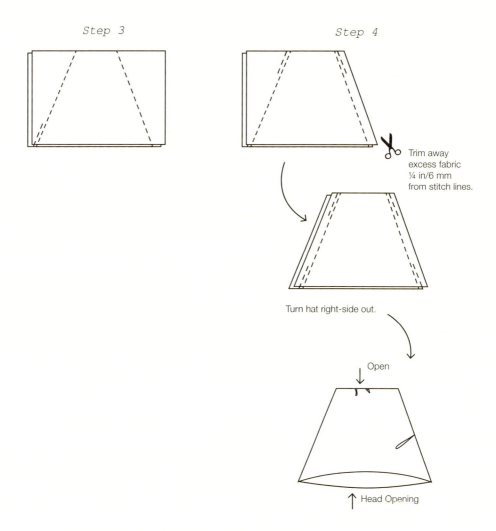

Step 3

Step 4

Trim away
excess fabric
¼ in/6 mm
from stitch lines.

Turn hat right-side out.

Open

Head Opening

5. Lay the Hat Bow pattern piece out on the fabric scrap, with the fabric right-side up. Pin the pattern piece down, and cut around it with fabric scissors. Remove the pattern piece and pins.

6. With the fabric hat bow, tie the top of the hat closed with a knot. Cut the strip to the desired length.

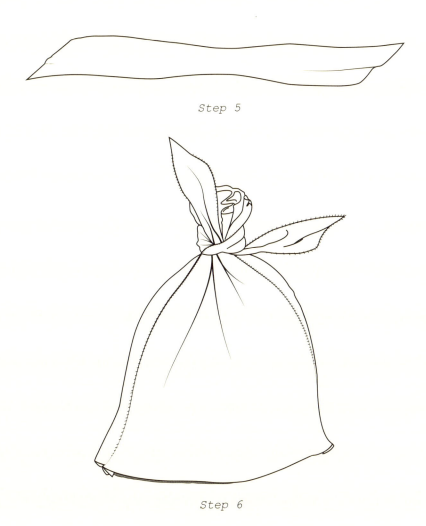

Step 5

Step 6

Apron

Aprons and rag dolls just go together. There are dozens of ways to mix up this design so you can make a whole collection of aprons— it's really all in the details. Because of the size, aprons are my favorite place to use a small scrap of antique trim or lace for detail. These aprons look nice with any outfit.

Materials

Apron Pattern (provided at the back of the book)

$^1/_4$ yd/23 cm of solid linen or cotton print fabric

Coordinating thread

Small piece of antique trim or lace (optional)

Tools

Pencil or tailor's chalk

Tracing paper

Paper scissors

Straight pins

Ruler

Fabric scissors

Sewing machine

Small scissors

Iron and ironing board

$\longrightarrow$

1. Using the pencil and tracing paper, trace the Apron Pattern.

2. Using the paper scissors, cut out the Apron pattern piece.

3. Lay down the fabric right-side up, making sure the fabric selvedge is at the bottom. Place the pattern on the fabric, and secure with straight pins.

4. Using the pencil, trace on the fabric around all outer edges of the pattern. Using the fabric scissors, cut out the Apron piece.

5. Using the pencil and ruler, draw an 18-by-1³/₄-in/46-by-4.5-cm rectangle (for the waistband tie) and a 1¹/₂-by-1¹/₄-in/4-by-3-cm rectangle (for the pocket) on your fabric. Cut out the rectangles with the fabric scissors.

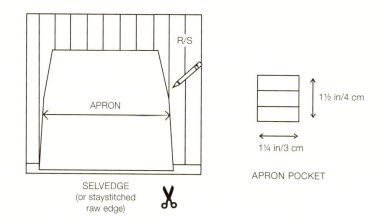

APRON POCKET

APRON WAISTBAND TIE

Steps 3–5

The Making of a Rag Doll

6. With the sewing machine, attach the pocket to the apron, sewing $1/8$ in/3 mm in from the pocket edge around three sides. Reinforce the beginning and end of the pocket seam with back-stitches. Staystitch both side edges of the apron $1/8$ in/3 mm in from the cut edge, and reinforce the beginning and end of the stitched line with backstitches.

7. Set the sewing machine to baste (the longest stitch setting). Baste a stitch line $1/4$ in/6 mm from the top edge of the apron, leaving long thread ends before and after basting. Gently pull on the threads like a drawstring to make gathers in the fabric. Gather the top of the apron to a total width of $3^1/2$ in/9 cm (the original width was $4^1/2$ in/11 cm).

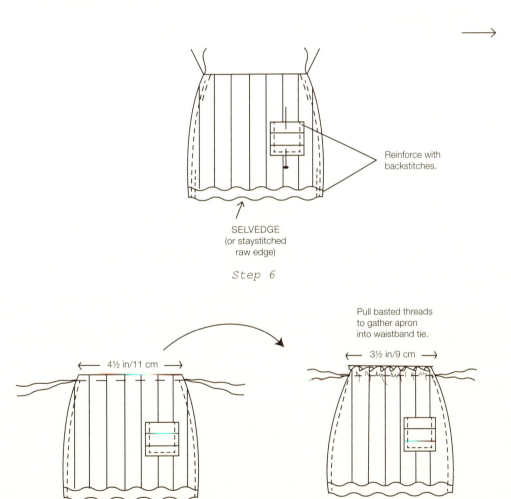

Reinforce with backstitches.

SELVEDGE
(or staystitched raw edge)

Step 6

Pull basted threads to gather apron into waistband tie.

$4^1/2$ in/11 cm

$3^1/2$ in/9 cm

Step 7

8. Fold the apron waistband tie in half lengthwise and measure 1³/₄ in/4.5 cm from the center on each side of the fold. Using the small scissors, make a tiny ¹/₈-in/3-mm clip on each side to mark the placement of the gathered edge of the apron.

9. Between the clip marks, pin the gathered apron to the waistband tie, right-sides together, with the top edge of the apron lined up with the bottom edge of the waistband tie. Adjust the sewing machine stitch to sewing length (medium-small), and sew a line over the basting stitches used for gathering.

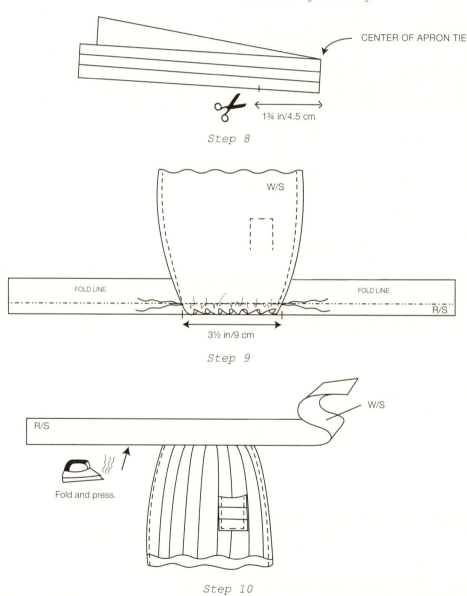

CENTER OF APRON TIE

1¾ in/4.5 cm

Step 8

W/S

FOLD LINE

FOLD LINE

R/S

3½ in/9 cm

Step 9

W/S

R/S

Fold and press.

Step 10

The Making of a Rag Doll

10. Pull the apron down and, with the iron set on medium heat, press, allowing the edge of the waistband tie to fold under $^1/_4$ in/6 mm to the wrong side. Fold the remainder of this long edge of the waistband to the wrong side $^1/_4$ in/6 mm, and press.

11. Fold the waistband in half, wrong-sides together, and press. Pin the folded pressed waistband and edgestitch using a short stitch setting on your machine to finish the apron tie.

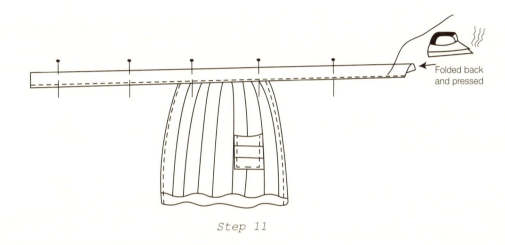

Folded back and pressed

Step 11

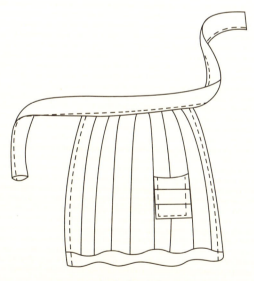

Finished Apron

My Favorite Sources

VINTAGE FABRICS AND NOTIONS

ADDISON ENDPAPERS
Amazing for trim, buttons, and antique treasures.
www.addisonendpapers.net

ALAMEDA ANTIQUES FAIRE
My number-one flea market.
www.alamedapointantiquesfaire.com

ATOMIC GARDEN
An inspiring, well-edited shop.
www.atomicgardenoakland.com

CHELSEA ANTIQUES
A favorite of mine. I have filled my home and studio with finds from them.
www.patscountryantiques.com

ERICA TANOV
Offers a perfect assortment of antiques and bohemian textures.
www.ericatanov.com

FOG LINEN WORK
A great place for linen pieces that has a utilitarian vibe.
www.foglinenwork.com
www.shop-foglinen.com

KNITTERLY
Amazing yarn shop. I source all my yarns and embroidery floss here.
www.knitterly.net

LIBERTY OF LONDON
Famous for their iconic florals and patterns.
www.liberty.co.uk

MAUDE RAREFINDS
An eclectic collection of treasures.
www.maudeshop.com

MERCHANT AND MILLS
Offers high-quality tools and notions. Filled with an old-world sensibility.
www.merchantandmills.com

NEST
Specializing in French antiques, this shop has a great assortment plus fabrics and prints.
www.nestsf.com

PAPIER VALISE
A good source for tags, papers, and office supplies.
www.papiervalise.com

SELVEDGE DRYGOODS
Inspiring magazine and shop
revolving around textile
history and artisans.
www.selvedge.org

SIENNA ANTIQUES
A wonderful antique shop filled
with large industrial pieces.
www.siennaantiques.com

SUMMERHOUSE
A well-edited shop with
antiques and artisan pieces.
www.summerhouse57millvalley.com

TALE OF THE YAK
Focuses on paper art and
special treasures.
www.elmwoodshop.com/stores/
tailoftheyak.html

TINSEL TRADING COMPANY
Beautiful notions and findings.
www.tinseltrading.com

BLOGS

Blog.piajanebijkerk.com
I love to see what catches
her eye.

Emmas.blogg.se
Totally inspiring home
interiors.

Remodelista.com
A resource for finding new
artisans. Inspiring interiors.

Themakersproject.com
Interesting artisan profiles.

BOOKS

Simply Scandanavian
Edited by Sara Norrman

Handmade Home
by Mark and Sally Bailey

Amsterdam: Made by Hand
by Pia Jane Bijkerk

*Zona Home: Essential Designs
for Living*
by Louis Sagar

Chanel
by Andrew Koda and Harold
Bolton

Etcetera
by Sibella Court

*A Perfectly Kept House Is
the Sign of a Misspent Life*
by Mary Randolph Carter

Acknowledgments

I am constantly in awe of the amazing team with which I get to work. The amount of care, intention, and grace with which you all approached this project has inspired me!

Thanks to my lovely editor at Chronicle Books, Laura Lee Mattingly, for giving us the opportunity to create this book (and, of course, for keeping us on track!). Thank you to the rest of the team at Chronicle, Jennifer Tolo Pierce (art director), Doug Ogan and Marie Oishi (managing editors), Lindsay Sablosky (production manager), and Lorraine Woodcheke (publicist). Thank you to Charlotte Bird and Paige Thomas for interpreting my sketches and thoughts into patterns others can follow. To Tristan Davison for perfectly capturing with his camera all that I surround myself with to feel creative. Kim Hillman, thank you for going down the constantly winding road of this project and navigating every turn with ease. And for doing truly everything to pull this book together! Thanks to the entire atelier team who have been so supportive during the project. And most important, to my loves Erio, Stella, and Tiger: Thank you for your patience, love, support, enthusiasm, and creativity.

Index